Tamarind and Mango Women

Poetry by

Opal Palmer Adisa

Sister Vision

Black Women and Women of Colour Press

ISBN 0-920813-71-2

1992 © Opal Palmer Adisa

Canadian Cataloguing in Publication Data

Adisa, Opal Palmer

Tamarind and Mango Women

Poems
ISBN 0-920813-71-2

I. Title

PR9265.9.A35T3 1991   811   C91-095052-0

Cover, Book Design & Production: Stephanie Martin
Printed and bound in Canada by Union Labour

Many of these poems were previously published in *The Daily Gleaner*, Kingston, Jamaica, 1976 -1978; *Caribbean Poetry Now* edited by Stewart Brown and Mervyn Morris; *Voice Print* edited by Stewart Brown, Mervyn Morris and Gordon Rohlehr; *Making Face, Making Soul,* edited by Gloria Anzaldúa; *The Caribbean Writer; New England Review and Bread Loaf Quarterly.*

Published by:
Sister Vision Press
P.O. Box 217
Station E
Toronto, Ontario
Canada M6h 4E2

*To Catherine James Palmer, my mother,
whose independence, assurance, determination and
love can be traced in many of these poems.*

These poems were written between 1974 - 1990.
Written in Jamaican Dialect and Standard English, they
reflect the fusion of the two languages that is so common
with the Jamaican people.

CONTENTS

TAMARIND

MANGO WOMEN

TAMARIND

A Cultural Trip

Press me to your bread-fruit chest;
enfold me in your mango arms;
kiss me with those shoe-black lips;
let me taste your guava sip.

Be my father forgotten in cane-fields;
my brother hidden under banana bunches;
my son killed by election promises;
be my Rasta-man who dreams of the promised land.

Hold me in the fallen chambers of Port Royal;
caress me on the slopes of Dunn's River Falls;
take me on the white sandy beaches of Negril.

Come to me
be mine to love
over and over again.

Sunday Songs

De chick break
open it's shell
de dog spin
in a circle
snappin at sand-flies
Cricket time:
de fast-bowler drive bat connect wid ball
cheers awaken from de bleachers
SIX!
Another batsman born

Sister Joyce
busy makin
sandwiches and coffee
Bertram mule
kick him in de behind
Harrison doze

L.B.W. — leg before wicket
argument
Errol run onto field
wid water fi de umpire
de sun recede
behind de hill
mosquitoes buzz
Tea-time

De Thomas'
finish dem gungu-rice-an-peas
& chicken wid carrot juice dinner;
pickney bearin
hymnals, dressed in dem Sunday best
wid ice-mint and snow-ball sweets
pushin out their cheeks
dogs ride each other
pickney dem point and giggle
cricketers leave fields,
spectators play ball
Duggie roll de ground smooth

Cookie collect eggs
from her fowl-coop
Ettie breast feed and breed
another pickney

De moon is out
an owl hoot;
eheh!
Who dead dis quiet
Sunday evenin?
Dacas has another boy
de dog sleep
pan de front step

Will the Real Island Please Stand Up

De grass
is no longer green
de palm trees are dead
de sea is full of weeds
and de white sandy beaches
are covered with rubbish

Eight year old girls
stand by Carib Theatre
late night show begging ten cents;
in Ocho Rios straw-makers
argue with tourists
arms akimbo
hands a flailing
"yuh come from rich America
come tief me off"
Negril women show their navels
buy panties for dem daughters,
still I can't leave
connected through birth pains
this island of tamarind and mango

Went Down Town One Night

I
Bajans are like me
fashioned after the night
illuminating like stars
twangy lilt — somewhere between
de teeth and throat

She say
"if a see yuh flirt
ah will fly back mi wrist
an wine,
mine a shame yuh"
Friendship
we stare
search beneath
skin

See us on Baxter road:
grandma by de bar
swinging she hips
de rhythm change
she shake she shoulder

At de shop
papa, an old sage
stand upright
him salt beard
restin on him chest
twenty-five years he

livin on Baxter road
studyin his people
dem frown and grimace
de laughter of dem walk
de fatigue and rejection
springin from dem breasts,
fallin into de gutters
like water from de
stand-pipe, de communal
meetin place for de women and children
A youth man tows him girl-friend
pon de bar of his bicycle;
she is all smiles
We slummin
lickin our fingers from Bajan fish
she peppa to warn,
to tease, to have fun,
to say a waan yuh man
Swap comfort fah poverty
we head for Slims' bar

II
Inside, he reaches
for my hand,
sits close, rubs shoulder
as he sips on his beer,
drags on his cigarette;
he nudges
I turn into his face
and from somwhere
in his eyes
words:

"I'm attracted to you"
touch me like old, old times
I smile before
turnin to the scene
on the bandstand/dance-floor:

Mr. Drum Stick
polyester, white down
shoes and socks
is blowin away the denial
of himself: one hand on de key board,
de other fingerin de notes of his horn —
Jazz, Bajan style
with Mr. Checkered Shirt,
plaid pants, touch off
with a two toned brown & beige shoes,
foot-steppin with a white rootupus*.
It's Slims' where
the French cement workers
hang out to pick up
poor Bajan girls
and suck on their pollens
Euro-Canadian-American rootupus
livin in color her black-stud fantasy
buys herself a boy,
who permits her to rub on him
allows himself to rub on her
his face taut de muscles
drawn stiff, tight like a condom
over an erect penis
the yankee dollar!

Queen rootupus
does not smell de hate she baits
intent on battin she eyes,
swingin she hipless waist,
shakin she saggin shoulders
in a Mae West exaggerated pose.

De boy's face remains taut
knife sticks from his back pocket;
he gwine use it to slice her up
after sellin himself
recoilin from de touch
of she lobster flesh.
Such a mango skin Bajan youth
him eyes no longer see
closed up elsewhere
in de bosom of his brown mama
who hasn't a penny to replace
dis survival dance

III
His fingers play
with mine, relieve the pain
tellin me in warmth
that he too is suffocatin
from these sisters & brothers
of our, their lives
like nine days piss in a pot.
Charred by de laughter
of these passive participants
we laugh our belly laugh,
takin the pain into our stomachs,

appplaudin dis crop-over dance
that simply refuses
to get done.

Rootupus - a West Indian term meaning trashy or slut-like

Egypt Calls

When ribbons hung
in my hair
I sat under
the poui tree
whose branches extend
like arms umbrellaing
the land while my uncle
painted in oil the
house on the hill.

We sang praises
said we would redress
knew her when she
and Ethiopia were the continent
when Nefertiti
played by her pyramids
and Tutankhamen slept in
her arms.

All that time we dreamed
and felt her sand between
our toes.

Voices Refrain

Divine Comedy is about a people in search of something to believe in when they are trapped in poverty, fear and prejudice. They follow a false prophet for a time but when he is killed, they turn to strength in themselves for guidance and faith — OWEN DODSON

African people
have eaten
winter too long

Women's tongue
go click-clack
ohmeohmy

Men's eyes
make plural incantations

Brothers and sisters
carry rum of their ancestors

Children
dance a medley
come carnival

Anarchy!

Nzinga/Cudjoe/Grannie Nannie/
Biko/Toussiant/Nat Turner
their steps rope our necks

Women's knees
are painted green
bleeding
until Namibia and Soweto
are *Milkman

African people are mask
that do not tell a story
but idealise it

Men shave their pubic hair
they laugh
flies follow them

No more weeping
echoes the deaf woman
my ears filled with wax
enough rivers
and what of warts for eyes
says he who vanquished sight
I grew sick of our noses and mouths
a fire-works of colours
I made soup

Apart
clap the women
Apart
snap the men
Apartheid
mime the children
making a game of it

words are jingles
catch a ...
by his toe
apart together/apart/together
heid/heid
where do we draw the line
we drink their wine
cut our words on their machines

The chorus is a litany
of adjectives divided
by semi-colons & questions

Commas lead from libation
to ancestors
songs are exclamations
songs are Namibia
the circle
is mud-packed wall
push a bone through your ear
stretch your lips
carve your face
divination
Ibo/Ashante/Mandingo
cremated

African people
have eaten winter
too long
much too long
their torsos diamonds

arms bauxite
heads nutmeg
legs pitch-lake
lips full
nose wide enough
to breathe

Colons & apostrophes
are sucking
Namibia/Jamaica/Grenada/Nicaragua
trees their bark stripped
puppeteer pulls string
waist bands
vomited up
by metropolis

History is
symbol on paper
African people
cough up clay designs

Apart/heid
double-dutch

Holocaust

Milkman is a character in Song of Solomon *by Toni Morrison*

Feeding

Sometimes
this need
to remember what's
between my legs
to mention
terrible back pains
at that
certain time of
the month
of daggers
in my anus
when desire isn't met
and a warm body
in the bed
takes precedence
over ideals
but I mustn't
discuss such things
in public
ladies aren't supposed
to be in touch
with that space
their thighs
try to hide
but I never said
I was a lady

Koo* De Man

Koo De Man!
see yah jesas
De Man naked as de day him born.

Koo him tings swingin
from side to side like
horse tail a fan fly.
Him poor mama mus wish him dead
sheself dead an de whole society.

Unnu come look pan
De Man stark-starin naked
ah walk pan Kingston Street.
De pickney dem eyes jus ah
feast pan him tings
like bees pan sugar cane.

Run guh cova De Man tings
Lawd! madhouse full

Wha wrong wid de society eh?
Wha do eeh?
Wha mek people mus mad
galang an nubody pay
dem mind.

De society ahfi tap
hold debate an check
its disease.

*Koo - look at

A Wind is Blowing

What have
I sown
photographs
from image
to picture
all smiles
but there is none
here tonight

Turn the page

I reach out
the air
comes up tasteless
I can't eat chalk
any longer
I plant
not just shells
at times
my needs are a cough
trapped in my tonsils
I crave warmth
my nouns and verbs
don't embrace me
I'm teaching them
but they are slow
humming:
"There's nothing like
the real thing.."

Where are the photographs
of swollen eyes
quivering lips,
vacant rooms
with only empty spaces
to fill them?
I eat need like jelly
sometimes it shoots
from me like feces.

Memories,
experiences
why don't they talk?
Images leave me
hungry.
I can't touch them
or feel their breaths
I want smells
to fill my room
soft and hard sweats

Words to touch skin
to swallow saliva
I need pictures
that have
headaches and diarrhea
when only blank walls
speak back to me.

The Drum is the Heart

The drum
beats us onward

Kinfolks
in Africa-land
do you mourn us
all us sold for profit,
all us kidnapped
to spread throughout
the rest of the world,
all us thrown over-board
to avoid fines
all us bartered
for rum, beads and oranges.

The drum
beats...

Kinfolks
in Africa-land
I have been singing
your songs,
nursing my wounds
to come to you pure
but you
who were not
swapped for trinkets
do you mourn us
pour libation
go on pilgrimage

to the ocean and ask Yemoja
to protect us?
Do you weep for those of us
sacrificed
to share our spirituals, blues & odes.

The heart
beats...

Kinfolks in Africa-land
seek us,
make sacrifice for us,
pay homage
in remembrance
that some of us
were traded
so that all of us
would continue.

The drums
carry our spirits home
beat on drums
beat on hearts.

Cane Cutters

Bursting canes
led astray by breeze
that carries them like
raised skirts.
Cane fields of fecund
ebony skin women,
breasts hard with milk
seep freely into day.
Joy plaited in stalks.
Sweat propagates soil.

Machetes hoisted/lowered
Cane tossed on heap.
Faces starched indifferent.
Eyes buried into the earth.
Only bent backs and raggedy
stained handkerchieves
worn with perspiration
cling to heads.
Songs appear monotonous
but to those familiar
with the notes of burden.

Words echo from sugar-sap
Sun umbrellaing
adds to curse, yet steers
bodies in motion.

Wagons loaded!
Tons of cane carried along
narrow, dusty roads
leaving passengers
scattered feeding puss-filled sores.
Wasps, buzz-around
suck at succulent sweets.

Bent bodies revert.
Bowels are clamorous.
Stained handkerchieves
wipe sweat, odor.
Donkey borne with load
bray-marches
a straight line of labor.
Lunch: Number-Eleven mangoes,
sardine glued between cooking-butter
on thick chunks of Hard-dough bread
washed down with sweet water.

Boy-child feeling manhood
in his crotch
hops wagon/steals sugar.
Slips!
Wheels get hold of leg,
grinds flesh into dust.

Returning
swarm of bees!
One of their feet
part of the earth.
Cane borne on heads.

Cane, step-child strapped
to sides;
wagons loaded.
Another journey begins
and faces of drunken smiles
become pattern rolled
by wagons' wheels.

Cultural Justification

People say,
"if de pickney good lookin
have qualifications
nuh red-eye
but still she nuh succeed
mus nega green eye an
bad mouth pon she"

So sittin unda de
bus-shed
writin and seein
people stare pon me
thinkin me fit fah belleview*
ah pray fah madness
so I can tell dem bout
dem rass and nuh gi a damn

belleview: Government-run mental institution in Jamaica.

De Country Grumbles

Bush! Bush! Bush!
All man see
is bush.
Every mornin
walk nearly mile fi
catch water;
water in bucket wet-up
me clothes.
Heavy bucket crushin
me brains.

Bwoy! Life hard sah.
Climb up hill, cut thru
track get up before daylite,
Duppy an Rolling-Calf
all through de nite
mek sleep hard.

Pit-toilet far
from house especially
since nite so dark.

Three miles walk
to school pon rough
gravel road wid no
shoes to cut de bruise.

Mama guh a river
fi wash we clothes.
Papa guh a bush

all day til nite an
when school time come
still nuh money
fi buy shoes

Two-cents
buy snow-ball
fah lunch; home-work
by lantern lite.
A thatch-roof hut
from coconut boughs,
corn-meal dumplin an
mackerel again.
Country life nuh joy
me bwoy.

Ethiopia Unda a Jamaican Mango Tree

Jah Brown si-down
unda a mango tree
him anger
jus swell.

Babylon refuse
him wuk
cause him dreadlocks.

Him pull pon de weed
iflect Babylon gwine
meet fire I an I
son of Jah
I an I a guh
plough I land
I an I a guh eat fresh
vegetable no deadas. I an I
a guh mek dis mango tree
I temple. I an I a guh hook
till Jah come fi I.

But Jah Brown
nah frown,
cut no strut,
weed cool him down.
Him eyes lost in smoke.

Ethiopia! Ethiopia! Ethiopia!
Ring in him ears
Jah Brown arrives at
Haile Sellasie's palace

Is given a red cloak,
fresh fruits,
marries a queen.
Him spirit
soar.

Jah brown wipe spittle
from him chin.
Raised arms held to
de sky,
  "I an I is son of Jah
  I an I is Jah
  I an I is Prince among Princes
  I an I is."

Jah Brown nah
cut no strut
him just si-down
unda Jah mango tree.

Tamarind

Mangy dog
mingle wid pot-belly
pickneys;
leaves sail
in open gutters

Human feces
is de only
refuse in garbage bins
Johncrows* circle

Women at darkness
keep company
wid streets, leanin against
walls, waitin men whose
wallets mean food
Tamarind switch
slices flesh
Johncrow descends

Johncrow - a large, black carnivorous bird; vulture

Count Ossie

I saw you perform
your pearly smile
danced at me.
Mother Africa does well by her men
who keep close to her bosom

Now we speak of honor
we sing
but only you know de rhythm

Play Count Ossie
play de drums...
the telephone of Africa
play
while you journey home

De drums bawl out sufferation
dem rejoice, dem bawl
dem sound for you Count Ossie.
Play de drums.

Superstition

Rollincalf
wid heavy chain,
drippin blood
roam at nite.
Only Biggar wid
him left hand
can still dis calf-duppy*

Last nite
when Miss Pearl
returnin from market
Hog-an-sow
took afta she;
good ting she had
a box of matches;
she strike three sticks
throw two weh, hide
de third in she mouth

Crosses tek
me sista de odda nite:
she thought it strange
when first she see
a saddle by de road
den little further on
a man wid a bucket
but not a sign of life
from de man
but when she tun de next bend
and spot de horse

and memba she granny warnin
she tek off
and good ting too
Tree-Foot-Horse
almost run she down
still she nuh believe
duppy deh
say is country people
wid dem stupidness
country so dark
any little ting fly bout
like leaf or peenywally*
is duppy
me ask she why she bruk
she neck de odder night
when Three-Foot-Horse
chase she
she say
"is tired me did tired
mek me run go cover up
in me bed."

Duppy - ghost, spirit
Peenywally - fire flies

People First

The river
no longer purges
the land every monsoon

Again the rain comes
and another life is washed away

Children
filled
with water
begrudge every crumb
that falls

The fruits of Africa, Haiti, Guatemala
and the Phillipines
are left to become
bones

Garbage-bins of the west
over-flow
porpoises, whales, seals and dogs
get coverage on prime-time
not the war
against hunger

Inverted

Never thought
of roots
in California
never thought
about African women
here
long before slavery
proud ruler

Califia
African woman
purple/black
beautiful
Califia amazon leader
warrior
governed Baja California
in Cortes' time

Now you
are forgotten
Califia
you are painted
a colour that's not
reflective of your heritage
your name is no longer
chanted by black children
Califia
African woman
amazon
like Cleopatra

and many of our great people
you're painted white
and we are not
taught about you
real and African
one of us
Oh Califia

De Extra Dollar

Because times
are hard
and man and woman
must put bread
in them stomach
words get lost
trampled on
by the eight to four
dollar in de pocket
survival

De spirit
is shunned
poetry becomes
luxury
but we keep de faith
you and I
holding words
as magic

Look For Poetry

I walk streets
invisible
to pedestrians
whose
gait I search
for poetry
knowing the most powerful
wordsongs
come from
people's souls
that do not
imitate
society's
good-manners

People walk
more poems
are printed

De Boys

Four boys idle by de
run-down changing room
once reserved
for tourists
but de Jewel Movement
took back de people's land
ending dem exile —
servers of someone else's
dream vacation

De boys invite me
to snap dem picture
dem eyes clear as de blue
water through which I see
my toes wiggling in the
white sand

Poverty marks dem:
leathery soles
bruised knees
firm limbs
eagerness to please
to be acknowledged
dem attention
can easily be claimed

De revolution has
not yet found dese boys
strewn on the beach like
paper blowing in de wind

de complexities of socialism
are vague
offer dem money/work
any mercenary has a chance

Four boys on de leaf scattered beach
waiting ... waiting
for something to happen!

*Attack at Dawn

These are dangerous times.

There is no one within reach.

I am too far
away from home.

I am a slave.
This is the law of
the land.

The man who fathered me
is a tyrant
his rape of my mother
is celebrated.
This is the law
of the land.
I am holding
my breath;
my chest cracks and crumbles
under the strain

All my blood
is drained
They have killed my boy.
Maurice Bishop is dead.
Dead.
Dead.

Suddenly,
the meaning of my name
is a task.
The market is empty.
They have killed my boy.
Maurice Bishop is dead.
Dead!
Dead!

The yearning
for my name to pave roads,
water nutmeg
is brushed aside
like some idle fly.
My boy is dead.
I am a slave.
This is the law of
the land.

There must be another word,
synonymn
for pawn,
imperialism,
capitalism,
communism,
democracy.

Maurice
a man
helping us believe
we could govern
our own lives.

These are dangerous times.
I let out my breath:
sweat,splinter and bones
scrape my mouth.

My boy is dead.
Once more
we are roped
and battered.

**Attack at dawn refers to the invasion of Grenada
by U.S. troops on October 25, 1983.*

My Life

Mornings
I wash the matter
from my eyes
my mother roasts me
breadfruit to eat

My grandmother
hems my dress
that is my life
like who I vote for
and what I call myself

In my country
night
is a black coal
and day a
sun-flower
we understand
things without
having to classify them

Grandpa
doesn't understand
how sharing his yams
with his friend, Brother Joseph,
is communistic

Father says he has nothing
against "ISM's" capital or otherwise
but he tastes gall
when he sees people
living in card-board shacks
and digging through garbage bins
for food
and that is
an example of democracy

Where we live
is called
primitive, undeveloped
we are certain the naming
is significant
as our rules
are few and simple
we don't
harbor
liars
thieves
or murderers
they are as
hunger,
homelessness
and needing an ID
to be out
South Africa and
U.S.A. are synonymous

We Have It

The dream
began before
Africans were tracked
on the coast of Ghana
the Middle Passage
flesh for sharks

The dream started
before 1619
when the first slaves docked
before
we knew Mississippi
fed her blood
for passage
before Rosa Parks
the Montgomery Bus Boycott

The dream isn't
a singular vision
it lives in the Dozens
Second Line
Praline and Fat Tuesday
It's the beat of our walk
the slang of our tongues

The dream is us
we got it from old people's eyes
the way their fingers knuckle
the glee and laughter
of black children
starched and oiled for church

The dream lives
in sisters
their heads held sure
in brothers
their confident bop

We all have the dream
Martin Luther King, Jr.
gave it voice

I Remember Knowing You Intimately

for a very long time
i believed
you were invincible
and still today
you are indomitable

mommie i used
to call you
until at ten i challenged
you to call me daughter
you laughed at me
i retorted with cathy
and that's how we've
been since then
cathy
you mother
you father
you the world

i remember
over-hearing men
say
how you were
coco cola bottle
shaped in your
hobble shirts
i remembering
feeling proud
that you were desired
you — my mother

your face
always dancing
with laughter
your heart
always willing
your spirit
never broken

how did you manage
to be so relentless
so sure
so optimistic
can i tell you now
the consternation
dawn and i felt
when we lost
the twenty five guineas
for our preparatory school fees
but you never spanked us
i don't even remember you yelling
just said a way had to be found

mostly i remember
how easily
you dressed others
down with your tongue
your mastery of words
how everyone —
men and women
rich and poor
respected you
came to you for advice
asked you to be godmother

for their children
how generous
you were/are
sharing all you have
willing to teach
what you know
always doing
something

i wonder if
that's why
i'm always
going

mostly
i want to thank you
for being beautiful
daily
i sat between
your thighs
my elbows and arms
resting on your knees
my head sometimes
cradled on your thighs
and as you talked
and plaited my
hair i knew
from the love you
brushed into my hair
i was beautiful
and had every reason
to be proud

So Soon
(for Tarik)

i'm locked
in your gaze
which reaches
beyond
what is
my soul

so soon

i have
surrendered
myself
to you

so soon

no part of me
is secret
i've led
you to the deepest
crevices

so soon

be gentle
i could break
at the slightest
disregard

Go On Miss Big Lady

so you're
five
grown
growing
wanting to know
what i'm going
to be when i grow-up
maybe i'll be like you
or maybe i'll be shy
more reserved

you speak for
both of us
sometimes too bossy
most times too defiant
always resilient
spirited
but i must teach
you to admit
what you don't know
i must help you
to harness your energy
and temper your enthusiasm
i must teach you pride
yet show you that humility
can be a crown of glory
i must love you
fiercely
but help to guide
you to use all your potential

i must be your advocate
coach   cheer-leader
mother and friend

miss five year old
grown lady
slow down...

People Walk

in
each gait
is a song

the muscles
the ligaments
the joints
the phalanges
flat-footed or
toe-ball contact

each proclaim
a beat
an inner
lark
that moves
us forward

A Remark

these poems
are legs and
breasts
braids and
high behinds

they've
walked on
broken bottles
drunk poinsettia milk

they are
grafted seeds
avocado pear
buttery and green
navel orange
sweet and seedless

enter these poems
they are the
residue of food
caught between teeth
the sweet taste
of dew on a leaf

their rhythms
are so sensuous
they titillate

Kilimanjaro

wake up
you gigantic brute
how dare you slumber

i flew across
two continents
rose at five a.m.
crossed two borders
travelled cramped
for five hours
to find you dozing
your head wrapped
from the cold fog

this is july
this is africa
the land of the sun
i want to see you
kilimanjaro
don't hide your head
in the smokey clouds
i need to salute you

tanzania, july 1986

Just a Touch

where to begin
to put sense
to the need
there are
60 seconds
in a minute
60 minutes
in an hour
he lived through
everyone of
those seconds
86, 400 in a day
1, 314 000 in a year
35, 478 000 in
twenty seven years

where to begin

baba mandela
i apologize
for all the times
i shunned my husband
over something trivial
baba mandela
forgive me
for all the times
i could have held
my children
but worried
about pampering
them

baba mandela
i am guilty
for not always
being thankful
for each day
i went where i wanted
saw who i knew
said what i thought

i'm still
trying
to understand
keeping faith
in twenty seven years

even in days
i cannot
hold it
there are 7 days
in a week
30 days in a month
365 in a year
9, 855 in
twenty seven years
still too many days
for me to carry
around
in my purse
only 3285 days
less than
i've been living

baba mandela
i drink
of your faith
that cannot
be measured
in seconds
or days
or years

just where
to begin

Just Like a Sister

just like a sister
to forget
who she is
vulnerable
her need
underscored

just like a woman
to give all her
strength to someone
else

just like a sister
to drape her body
in blue
get lost in singing
the blues
moaning of dreams
never realized
oh sister billie holiday
lord girl bessie smith

just like a woman
to fall in love
with a no counting fool
and abandon all her senses
sister-child why you
want to play
that old tired role
just like a sister

you   me
and all the rest
dressed in black
to bury our dead
endurance our crown
dependability our shield

just like a woman
just like a sister
just like a mama
always there
with words
that mask failure
and a smile
that's a genuine
welcome

yeah
just like a sister
a woman   you

Work

i'm the means
to someone's
wealth

hustle
bustle
pretend involvement
the work must be done

there was a beginning
maybe
a car
a house
a trip
the reason gets
more vague
beyond reach

coffee sustains me
the hands of the clock
move slowly

free at last

tomorrow already

no end in sight

Balloon Bouquet

early mornings
before
my eyes
open
chirping birds
whistling wind
wake me

through
my window
down in the courtyard
the coconut of africa
the curry of india
the saffron of quebec
the ketchup of america
are the children
playing
their arms and legs
in flight
their shrill screams
their laughter
soar in the air
balloons
i watch sailing
in the sky

No Apologies

my demands
did not force
you to lie

your mama
did the best
she could
to raise you
alone

grow up
away from your pain
it's not my womanhood
that snares you

Opening the Door Before Exiting

when i said
to myself
this isn't
what i want
the undoing
became less
traumatic
the search
more challenging

cowards live
on nostalgia
each new bud
stores its
own fragrance
and i learned
that adieu
leads to welcome

Liberation Coming

holler loud
voodoo drums blare
jean-claude duvalier
has flown the coop
baby-doc days are done
the tonton macoutes
are scattered
grains for fowls
to swallow

dambala old man
rout out the tyrant
dambala old man
rouse the people

no more
blood for sale
no more jeans
sown for dimes
no more
shoes mended
for nickels
voodoo drums cry
dambala old man
shaking his cane
1804 reenacted
toussaint announces
the ceremony
baby-doc gone
voodoo drums holler
liberation coming
coming around the bend...

Dem Talk But Dem No Know
What Dem Speak

jamaican men say
"woman is shadow
and man is arrow"

how many arrows
hit de target

maybe
this is de emptiness
between women and men

jamaican men
fraid fi give
of themselves
dem have to protect
themselves
against hurt
shame face
and separation
but dem gwine have
to relearn
to open up
if dem ever hope
to discover
dem manhood

We Dress Up

chances are
you've heard
about our flair
our knack for
getting dressed up
to prance, scintillate
and outshine
stars and honoured guests

we dress up
for funerals
weddings
and christenings
we dress for the postman
the bill collector
the bailiff
we dress up
spending time
to gloat about
who's wearing what
and who's hanging out with whom
we dress up
get all spiffy
and righteously clean

ain't no big thing
just our daily fling
oohing and aahing
applauding and serenading
accepting accolades
and recommendations
all dressed up...

A Run-Away

rain
washes out tracks

water
bleaches out smell

night
rest until dawn

sounds travel
conceal deed

sing those songs
that tell us
when to run

eyes to the sun
feet to the moon
run away children
abort fear

trees are beds
that nestle phantoms
trees are food
that direct us
to the river
run children
run
rain falling
run children

run
let your
rope-muscled legs
snake the water
run children
run
let your beating
hearts
propel you forward

you're almost there now
run
you're almost home
remember
the foot
with toes missing
remember
the back
brutalized with scars
remember the arm
that's now a stump
run children
run

water bleaches
scent
night rinses
plans

run
remember your way
back to yourself

We are Formed from Volcanoes

jamaica
is not south africa
although a black elite
rules
the poor man
and the rich man
rub shoulders

the boy
who keeps their pool clean
and their garden manicured
must watch their son
while he swims
but he's forbidden
to join him
they are both
black
jamaica
is not south africa
minimum wages
are in effect
blacks   browns
and whites
fraternize
decorum foreign
dress western
speech imitation

she's a live-in
rises at 6 am to

prepare their breakfast
clears the dinner table
at 7 pm
irons a dress
for the misses at 9 pm
for good wages
her mother keeps
her child
worker and employer
are black female mothers
jamaica
is not south africa
down the road
from a million dollar
home equipped with
a satellite dish
three colour tvs vcr
and swimming pool
is a shack with no
indoor plumbing
ten to two rooms
but dem lazy
dem lack ambition

jamaica
is not south africa
independence
is celebrated
every august 6th

How to Write the Poem of the Pebble
(for kamau e. brathwaite)

i must
remember
the seas that i crossed
i must face
this voyage
without shame
i must
claim
this land
that is now
my home
i must
remember
the death of the amerindians

my birth
was smeared with blood
other than my mother's
the pebble
was pressed
between their toes
so the lie
could be enforced
now i
must catch the water
in my mouth
use its salt
to embalm me

until each wave
that i stumble out
of writes
the poem
that breathes
through my mouth

MANGO WOMEN

Market Woman

Me wid
elephant
sappadilla
rear
walk tall
elegant
more poised
than vine-models
of Vogue

Fi me life-line
is not de whisper
delicacy of a rose petal
it tells de unyieldin
of de earth at times
of scrubbin
on rock's back
clothes stained with
guineps and aprons
marked with yams
of buffs on
a boy-child's back
growin
wid out a man

See dese breasts
heavin still firm
tauntin men's eyes
dey have nursed
seven pickney

and delighted more men
and is three man
did father me
seven pickney
and me did love all
of dem
no good as dem is
am I not
Granny Nanny
fightin
wid de Maroon
guerillas
am I not Cudgoe's
woman and Paul Bogle's
too
am I not de
same washer-woman
de one who cut cane
sweep road
and darn de defeat
in men eyes

Me wid
elephant's hide
still glare
stare
still get
photographed
by tourist
but wha
dem know
bout de Market Woman

before rooster crow
and mornin wash its eye
me roll me catta and
bear me fruit pon me head

De truck draw breaks
down Bredda Joe's shop
me mek haste
someone help me wid
me load

As de ride tun-tun
de fritters and fry plantain
pon me chest
me hope de pickney dem
get up fi guh school

Beverly mek dem tea
Keith full-up de drum dem
Jean and Carol sweep out de house
and Trevor and Peter sweep de dust
clean from in front de steps

De market: plenty
ants roastin pon coal,
barterin all around

But wha dem know
bout de Market Woman
whose lips spew froth,
cuss shit den
tun-roun and offer de cheeks

of she hide
Market Day
lady come buy fruits

Goweh yuh
face look like old rag hitch
pon barb-wire

Dem women who squeeze
dem foot inna spike-heels
and powder dem husband
absence, cyaan stan de
contented perspiration
of Market Woman

Goweh
barb-wire face
yuh husband ah sleep
wid me

Market Day, Market Day
lady come buy
fruits, come buy vegs
de Market Woman ah sell
dem cheap, come it's Market Day

The Rainbow

If we all knew where
we were going we wouldn't sit
on swings and hoist ourselves

up to meet cob-webs, if perhaps
we all stood as trees, babies
wouldn't be still-born and ice

cream wouldn't drip, and weddings
wouldn't take place in grave-yards
and children wouldn't scrape their

knees and Mitch up-stairs would be
able to play the piano and I wouldn't
bleed, if perhaps we all knew where

we were going I wouldn't need to write
I would till soil and the tap would
stop dripping so I could turn the radio

off and the air wouldn't hang like wet
waffles if we knew where we were going
there wouldn't be any place to go.

Usurption

Refusing
to taste
the saliva
of your foul breath
is as valid
as your craving
for flesh
given to you

But when you
plunge
spread raw fire
through me
even after
I scream no
then I want you
annihilated

In Kenya
rape carries
the death penalty

No, Women Don't Cry

In Africa, the saying is:
"A man is nothing without a woman
he cannot be a chief and when his breath
leaves him, his name
will be knocked into the earth
forgotten as his flesh."

So we women don't cry
we carry pain
in our bosom,
our stomachs bulge
pregnated by sorrow
we guard our tears
like a dam
for if we were to shed one drop
we couldn't stop
and we wouldn't have been able
to fight the Portuguese in the Congo,
the English in the Portland hills of Jamaica or
prisoners and derelicts of Europe in the Americas

If just one salt
had run down our cheeks
the pyramids would not be built
and the 60 million Africans
who drowned, starved and were killed
in the usurption of the continent—the middle passage
would not even be a memory

So women don't cry
we don't cry
mothers don't cry
when their husbands creep through the back door
while they remain with a stone stare
to sing freedom in the enemy's face,
sisters don't cry
when they see their brothers
strung up mutilated,
daughters don't cry
when a moment's rape
alters their future
no, women don't cry
we just hold it in
the crevices of our teeth,
in our wombs,
under our arm pits
in the loops of our ears
we women don't cry
we only weep and wail
in our rocking
that's why we talk to ourselves
and build more lives.

Sister to Sister

Sisters dance with each other
toss crinolines to Oshun
weave melons to Yemoja

When I see a sister
her mouth
touching the ground
her forehead a mud-cracked desert
I send her a sun-flower
making the dough within her rise
to push the door once more
of the downtown plantation high-rise zoo
we need new faces to wear
and friendlier places to display them

As earth mothers
we fan ourselves bonds
we walk upright
our goods borne
on our heads
we are as rain and stones
we sew wings
slice a piece of our bosom
for our offsprings
but we still must twist plaits
that no storm
can undo

When I see sisters
draped like Sheba's ship

a sail to Solomon
I applaud us
we daughters of Queen Hatshepsut
our legs are rivers
our arms weave moonsong
we bake   pound   grow muscles
and walk like cotton
Hey Sojourner
born Isabella
to remind us of our fists
and painted nails
our tongues are uranium
our eyes quicksilver
we are warriors
spit rolls off our backs
we swallow bullets using them
to fill the gaps in our walls
our houses need sticks
too long only twigs danced for us
Sister to mask-makers
three hands make merry
six make a wake
a multiple stood face to face
with the winds and made storm

We are soil and worms
and sweat and roots
we are women.

Mango Woman

The old adage reads:
familiarity breeds contempt
like salt stinging
eyes
too long I've worn
insecurity like goiters
long over-due amputation
forging
wanting to connect
my feelings
get treaded over

Now I'm on my own
my foot-steps
guide me
my voice
keeps me company
my needs roped into
a chord worn around
my waist

I will
cross
this desert
and dance
to the
oasis

Women At The Crossroad
(May Elegba Forever Guard The Right Doors)

I am a wandering child
etched in female palms
and male boots

By the window
I offered my breasts
but the vultures
took to them

Men and women
separate
like the
wrinkles of a bull dog
he leads
then I lead
painting similar landscapes
making babies
but not facing each other
who am I
who is he
this complement
that doesn't get
reckoned with
my breasts drip semen
his penis menstruates
we sleep
together
not touching toes

Equality has nothing
to do with love
it has everything
to do with power

I fear my wants
his are the drip
of a faucet
I maintain
that I am at once
victim and cypress
matriarch and whore
mother invincible
needing but unable
to receive
so I with
strength
worn as a banner
and he with
diminishing power
gets burned like the
Zulus!

Shame Ol' Lady

Eheh!
Watch de pickney dem nuh.
Dem a circle roun de Shame Ol' Lady bush
an a stretch out dem foot, dem hand
an a touch-touch she.

Watch how she shut-up she
eye tight-tight
an hide-hide she face

Shame Ol' Lady!
Shame Ol' Lady!
Wha shame yuh suh?
Tink me nuh know sey
a jilt yuh get jilted
mek yuh shame suh?

Poor Shame Ol' Lady.
De pickney dem jus a
tease — tease she suh.

Win or Lose How You Play It

No!
me nah call him
mek him tink me
a run him down.
No sah!
mek him galang.
But cho!
wha it matta
wha him tink
me a run him down nuh.

Hard fi
call man fi
come breathe hot air
pan me chest
him can call tuh.

*Macca Juck

"Wha appen gal?
hear seh
yuh get apartment."

Yes me chile
cyaan tek de modda
roof business.

Yuh know wha dem say:
Two ooman cyaan live
unda de same roof.

"Me know wha yuh
mean.
Fi me modda jus
watch-watch me every
move."

Suh how de dunnies?
Rent well steep!

"Ah dat now.
Force a gal fi hustle,
juggle two man
jus fi pay de rent.
Macca a juck me yes!
But wha fi do?"
MACCA JUCK EVERYONE.

*MACCA - *a sharp thorn*

Come See Dem Down By De River Wid Water In Dem Hem

Mundey marnin wash time,
wash dem clean,
wash dem bright,
Mundey marnin wash time
guh wash me dutty clothes

"Helllllo
Sister Joyce, Cookie, Dacas, Beverley,
Patsy how-de-do, how oonuh do?
Paulette how de pickney dem?
Wha appen Miss Mary?
me nuh see yuh a church yeseday.

"Collie-Face how married life?
how de husband a treat yuh?

"Wha appen Miss Pearl?
me hear de little one sick
yuh fi bun-out de room wid
frankincense
duppy a play wid de pickney.

"Eheh Miss Joyce
wha mek fi yuh
pickney dem mus
dutty suh much clothes?
look like yuh a wash
fi all a we an de river tuh.

"Me did see bredda Joe
a si down pan im veranda
jus now as me pass;
im strong yuh see;
should see im a clap
im jaw an a dip-dip im bread
inna im tea.

"But wait.
Who ever put dem bungle here
come tek it up.
Fi de las five years
ebery Mundey marnin me scrub
me clothes rite here pan dis rock."
"But look here Miss Pearl!"
dem gal
nuh know respect;
me jus dun change er diaper,
now she a tek man she
feel she can tek me rock.

"Listen gal, nuh vex me soul-case;
tek up yuh bungle an gwaan out me face.
See ere deh Miss Pearl;
de gal cyaan wash er drawers clean.

"Suh Miss Pearl, me hear seh yuh tek man!
tell me nuh; how it guh?
Mine! Yuh Missa Sam nuh tun
good inna im grave yet.

"Wash, wash, wash de clothes,
wash dem clean, wash dem brite,
me a guh wash de white one dem,
scrub dem pan de rock an lay dem
in de sun fi bleach;
me guh scrub de colored ones
den lay dem pan de bankin fi dry.

"Miss Joyce gi me some blue
me faget me blue a yard.
Miss Pearl gi me some space
me faget fi mend dis waist.
Wash-wash, Mundey marnin blues
Mundey marnin, Mundey marnin
Mundey marnin wash time."

Walking Away

As I grow to be
an old woman
I hide my breasts
guarding them from
men.

I lap my skirt
between my thighs
it is I alone who
stand to face the clock
what I seek
from men
is merely a dream

Discover Me
for Pam, Rosa and Joan

Needing someone
I love spread my legs;
I am weak,
I tear keep on tearing
stronger than men;
I die in the faces of boy children.

No one sees me,
only fertile bunches of banana.

No one knows
I am sap
which flows from cassava;

To get to me
peel away
and drink of my
juice

Madness Disguises Sanity

Sometimes
I mutter
as I walk
people
stare and pass by
on the far side

To be one
of those
desolate men
who lounge in
stink alleyways
forever talking
to the wind
their words
bullets
people shy from

But I am woman
conditioned
to nurse
my scream
like a mute child

So I write

They Come

I comfort
grief
at night
my pillow sags
with all the memories
I lie on it

I saw my man
trying despite
four o'clock bells
to put rice
on the table,
my man seized
for trying,
taken to the justice system,
tied to poles, flogged
like a criminal who
robbed and murdered the blind beggar

I watched puppets
whip my man
until urine
jutted from his penis
his ass cowered
but he didn't cry
I held back
my tears
So talk
those with rice and peas
and chicken on the table

but remember
I hold my head
talk to myself
I rock away images
to avoid wielding
the machete

Excuse Me But This Is Not A Love Poem
to Jimi

Sometime
I want to
be stem
solid steel
so I don't
break easily
on seeing you

Sometimes
I turn my cheeks
inside to be
a cactus in bloom
hoping you
won't touch me
prick your fingers
to bleed

Wanting you
spells not being
a fool
that's why
I shout it out
noise
drowns desire
and you're inside
my stomach
spasmodic

If I were sure
this isn't fancy
if I were certain
heat and sweat
make fire
my head would meet
you
locked as we are
in electricity

You
to Skip

> What I like
> most
> is turning
> hearing
> your even breathing
> and my
> nakedness
> touches your skin

Living and Hating
to L.H.

Rattle of the furnace
cooling
sounds of breathing
silence of the night
you left
children no longer
rejoice
innocence is a looking glass
continuous yearning
spilling of the soul
autumn when
laughter shone at our feet
the river was quiet
as we kissed
whispering
you in me
me in you

Wishing a child
would rise in
my uterus to
torment you
let you choose
but I am sensible
open about
what I want
afraid to gain what
I need

You come
I smile within
my breast
do you know
I already love
you for being here
night raps at the
bed for you
the mattress groans
Your pleasure
my desire
the walls listen
embarrassed
I chastise myself,
speak of throwing
mockery in your face
but you know
I come,
listen for
your call
and go foolish
Perhaps
I care
or maybe
I'm just lonely

Passion
to Shola, my daughter

When I'm
away from you
like I've been
these past weeks
I miss you beyond
thought

Often in my walks
your face appears
in my path
in conversation
with friends
a memory
of you in motion
flits across my mind
and I long desperately
to feel your arms
wrapped around my neck
to kiss your lips
to have you in my arms
so I ask myself
so afraid of this passion
I feel
how did I allow you
in less than two years
to become so gigantic
in my life

But
such a question
is folly

I miss you
who have become
the spectre in my life

Langston Hughs, Pablo Neruda, Aimé Césaire And Louise Bennett*

For all the
dreams deferred
I am singing
Protest Songs

As a little
brown girl
under sycamore tree
I dreamed of playing
hide-and-seek
in the pyramids

For all the dreams deferred
I am Returning
to my Native Land

Then a slender
young miss
with kinky plaits
I was Zenobia*
horseback riding
years kept piling on
womanhood
claimed me
yet my steps persisted
in reverberating

For all the
dreams deferred

Ah talkin
in me tongue

I look around
white-hair as I am
my back inclining
like the weather-beaten
palm trees
but my eyes dance
they dance
I sleep
with Tutankhamen
my sons and daughters
of Soweto are bold
I sing
keep all of myself
procreate
the dawn

I dance
this little brown girl
in the topmost branch
of the sycamore tree
dance and sing

Black American, Chilean, Martiniquian, and Jamaican poets

Zenobia A.D. 272, her empire, Palmyra stretch from the Euphrates almost to the Golden Horn and included Egypt and Syria. She took the throne after her husband's death.

Today's Grandmother
(A promise to my daughter Shola)

Sometimes
when we speak a word
repeatedly
it becomes lost
why we're fighting
somehow gets confused
with guilt

We're taught
to know the enemy
sometimes
the enemy
becomes so intimate
we become the enemy
of ourselves
our people

Do we know
whether we're engaged
in war/insurrection/revolution?

These are different
not merely semantics
replacement of corruption
for colour

Sometimes
we speak a word
not knowing

its meaning
so victory
doesn't begin
to be the sound of
Azania/Namibia
and people
over the world
are vomiting blood
to achieve

Out of the mountain
they came
carrying on their heads
whispers of words
told to them
generations and generations
ago

They were warned
some will come
claim then transmute
beware
friendliness killed
as stupidity
generosity stolen
as lack of need

Sometime
when we speak
a word repeatedly
meaning gets lost

Out of the forest
they came
dripping honey
to be ambushed
they were warned

I'm a mother today
twentyfive years
after tomorrow
I'll be a grandmother
rocking my daughter's children
on my knees
whispering words of
generations and generations
passed

I'll not disguise
spilled blood
bodies sprawled over Soweto
mats of grass for dogs to scratch
their fleas on
they were warned

Sometimes
we speak a word
not knowing the meaning

I'm not recounting
history
that
thing which
no longer lives

I'm not naming
atrocities
that which still happens
they were warned

Women deserve
the best or worst
of their men
sharing their beds
children need
the advantage or spoil
of a mother's hand
that sometimes sends
one's head spinning
or cradle one in comfort

They used to be warriors
not only men
women were bravest
they put food on tables

My grandchildren
are pulling my hair
their empty gums
suck my cheeks
imploring
no more no more
killings
no more no more
bantu land

Sometimes
when we speak
we speak a word repeatedly
and meaning gets lost

My grandchildren
are calling
no more no more
divide and rule
no more no more
sacrifice
no more no more
Biko/Winnie/Mandela
no more no more

Sing on sing on
sometimes
when we speak

Some other books by Sister Vision Press include:

Memories Have Tongue, poetry by Afua Cooper
dark diaspora...in dub, poetry by ahdri zhina mandiela
Piece of My Heart: A Lesbian of Colour Anthology, anthologised by
Makeda Silvera
Dry Land Tourist, short stories by Dianne Maguire
Nuclear Seasons, poetry by Ramabai Espinet
Remembering G and Other Stories by Makeda Silvera
Guyana Betrayal, a novel by Norma De Haarte
Creation Fire...An Anthology of Caribbean Women's Poetry edited by
Ramabai Espinet
Africa Solo, a play by Djanet Sears
Speshal Rikwes, poetry by Ahdri Zhina Mandiela
Lionheart Gal: Life Stories of Jamaican Women: Sistren with Honor
Ford-Smith
Silenced: Caribbean Domestic Workers Talk with Makeda Silvera
by Makeda Silvera
Blaze A Fire: Significant Contributions of Caribbean Women
by Nesha Z Haniff

1972